Special Bonus!

Want This Bonus Book for FREE?

Get <u>FREE</u>, unlimited access to it and all my new books by joining the Fan Base!

SCAN W/ YOUR CAMERA TO JOIN!

I AM CAPABLE OF ANYTHING:

1,500+ DAILY AFFIRMATIONS TO BOOST SELF-LOVE,
SELF-ESTEEM AND POSITIVITY

S. S. LEIGH

INTRODUCTION

My life hitting rock bottom is undoubtedly the best thing that has ever happened to me. I was so depressed and despondent that I became weary of having to carry on another day being so miserable. The truth was I wanted to be successful and happy but all the good things in life felt elusive to me.

There came a point when I became so tired of wallowing in self-pity and misery that I acquired the determination to turn my life around. The idea of not doing anything and staying miserable felt far more painful than taking action to improve my life. And so it began...

I started studying and practicing every possible thing that could help me improve my life. This is when I got introduced to the law of attraction - it began to suddenly dawn upon me how my deep-seated beliefs, ideas, and thoughts were shaping my 'reality.' I began to accept that I was the only one who was fully responsible for my experience of life so far.

Of course, it was painful to have a realization like that as it meant accepting that even the very worst things that had ever happened to me were my own doing. But I also felt empowered by this realization. If I could create a 'reality' I hated, then I could also manifest the life that I had always dreamed about but thought I couldn't have thanks to the programming I had received from teachers, society, and family.

I experimented with many different tools to transform my life – some worked, some didn't. My daily practice of affirmations is one of those tools that has created miracles in my life. If I couldn't keep my mind empty, then at least I could fill it with thoughts and ideas that would conjure me a favorable reality!

Once I started practicing affirmations every morning and evening, my life began to transform dramatically. I would say them out loud, write them down in a diary, and mentally keep chanting them throughout the day. It wasn't easy at first as my mind would often be overwhelmed with negative thoughts. I usually had to chant the affirmations out loud to quieten the din inside my mind. But, over time, the affirmations started being assimilated into my consciousness.

Later on, I even started taking extreme steps like recording the affirmations and playing them on repeat throughout the entire night. I started this practice because I learned that even when we are sleeping, our subconscious mind is awake. In fact, it is wide awake and easy to program or reprogram.

If you want to live the life of your dreams, then you have to be just as careful with your mental and spiritual diet as you are with your physical diet. This rule applies to both your waking and sleeping hours.

It won't be an exaggeration to say that practicing affirmations has changed my life. The only thing I wish I had at that time was some kind of guidance on how to practice them in an organized and structured manner. My practice of affirmations was chaotic at best. I used to jump from one affirmation to another – never delving deeply enough into one. This is why I have created this book.

HOW TO USE THIS BOOK

This is not a book that's meant to be read cover to cover in one sitting. You can read it like that if you wish but when it comes to the actual practice, you want to spend time with each set of affirmations that is assigned for the day. To unleash the real power of affirmations, you have to repeat them frequently throughout the day.

Spend at Least 5-10 Minutes Every Morning and Night Meditating on the Affirmations

Each chapter has 4 sets of affirmations – two for the morning and two for the night. I would strongly recommend that you set aside 5-10 minutes every morning right after waking up and 5-10 minutes every night immediately before going to bed. Use this time to dedicatedly practice your affirmations.

It would be best if you can do this in a quiet space where you won't be disturbed. Try to sit in a meditative position and take a few deep breaths to relax your body before starting the meditation practice. Once you start feeling relaxed, start repeating the affirmations that are assigned for that time of the day. You can do it quietly or you can say them out loud. You can also use a combination of both. Do what is most comfortable to you.

Write Them Down

There is a strong connection between the subconscious mind and the nervous system. While writing with a pen, the nervous system gets stimulated which, in turn, deeply embeds what is being written into the subconscious mind.

Hence, writing down the affirmations several times throughout the day can be a powerful practice for internalizing them. I would recommend that you do this at least 3-7 times for each affirmation. Of course, there is no upper limit to how many times you should be writing it. The more frequently you practice, the better it is.

Just make sure that you are doing it with all your focus and attention. Practice deep breathing to bring your awareness into the present moment and then start writing. You don't need to do this practice at a designated spot every day. Do it whenever you manage to find time in the day. You can even do it while commuting or when you are taking a break from work.

Keep Repeating Them Throughout the Day

Again, as I said earlier, the key to mastering affirmations is through repetition. The more frequently you repeat the affirmations, the more deeply embedded they get in your psyche.

Practicing affirmations shouldn't be something set aside for a specific time of the day. You can do it any time anywhere. There are no rules – only the ones that you make for yourself. If you enjoy saying them out loud, then do that. If you'd much rather practice them silently, then that's perfect as well. As long as you are practicing, you are improving. Don't try to wait for a perfect time or place to do it. Do it anywhere and everywhere!

Affirmations are especially helpful when you start feeling bogged down by negative thoughts. By focusing on repeating the affirmations, you automatically take the focus away from negative thoughts.

The bottomline is to make affirmations a way of life instead of an isolated practice reserved for specific times of the day.

DAY 1

MORNING AFFIRMATIONS

I accept myself exactly the way I am. I love myself unconditionally.
I am wonderful. I am amazing. I deserve the best in every situation.

EVENING AFFIRMATIONS

I trust that the Universe is working in my best interest.
I have faith in the process of life.
Tomorrow is a new beginning and I am ready for it.

DAY 2

MORNING AFFIRMATIONS

Today is a perfect day to be happy.
Today, I am committed to being my most radiant and joyful self.

EVENING AFFIRMATIONS

I honor the perfection of my body, mind, and soul.
Everything about me is perfect. I love myself.

DAY 3

MORNING AFFIRMATIONS

Today is my chance to begin again.
Today, I will focus completely on my own goodness.

EVENING AFFIRMATIONS

I am my own greatest fan and admirer.
I love myself for everything I am and all that I have achieved.

DAY 4

MORNING AFFIRMATIONS

I am worthy of love.
I deserve the best things that the world has to offer.

EVENING AFFIRMATIONS

I know how to get the best out of any situation.
I am wildly and massively successful at everything I do.

DAY 5

MORNING AFFIRMATIONS

The beauty of my soul is radiating through the perfection of my body.
I love and honor my body. It is the abode of my eternal soul.

EVENING AFFIRMATIONS

I trust that everything in my life happens in perfect divine timing.
I know and trust that all my dreams have already come true.

DAY 6

MORNING AFFIRMATIONS

All the love that I seek is within me.
I am at peace with who I am and where I am.

EVENING AFFIRMATIONS

I am releasing all beliefs, ideas, and memories that no longer serve me.
I know I deserve love and the best of what the Universe has to offer.

DAY 7

MORNING AFFIRMATIONS

Good things happen to me every day everywhere I go.
Every moment of my day is blessed with infinite abundance.

EVENING AFFIRMATIONS

I am loved. I am appreciated.
I support myself. I love myself.

DAY 8

MORNING AFFIRMATIONS

I enjoy taking care of my body.
It is easy for me to eat healthy and exercise regularly.

EVENING AFFIRMATIONS

I am beautiful/handsome and unique.
There is only one 'Me' in the entire world.

DAY 9

MORNING AFFIRMATIONS

I feel as fresh and vibrant as a flower in full bloom.
I am proud of how far I have come in life.

EVENING AFFIRMATIONS

It is easy for me to prioritize myself and my own needs.
I always have time to take care of myself.

DAY 10

MORNING AFFIRMATIONS

I choose myself.
I am my own best friend.

EVENING AFFIRMATIONS

I enjoy being the most amazing version of myself every day.
I am perfect. I am enough.

DAY 11

MORNING AFFIRMATIONS

I radiate peace and love.
Everyone loves me exactly the way I am.

EVENING AFFIRMATIONS

My heart is always open for giving and receiving love.
It is easy for me to love myself fervently.

DAY 12

MORNING AFFIRMATIONS

I am the most incredible person I know.
I deserve to be treated like a Queen/King.

EVENING AFFIRMATIONS

I choose peace and happiness.
I attract infinite abundance wherever I go.

DAY 13

MORNING AFFIRMATIONS

Everything is perfect in my world today.
I trust myself. I get the best out of any situation.

EVENING AFFIRMATIONS

It is easy for me to live a balanced and happy life.
I am grateful for the infinite abundance that surrounds me.

DAY 14

MORNING AFFIRMATIONS

I am powerful beyond measure.
I create my own reality.

EVENING AFFIRMATIONS

I am proud of the person that I am and the person that I am becoming.
I am my one and only competition.

DAY 15

MORNING AFFIRMATIONS

I have the power to turn all my dreams into reality.
I am happy and successful.

EVENING AFFIRMATIONS

I cherish and value myself.
Abundance flows to me from every possible direction.

DAY 16

MORNING AFFIRMATIONS

I choose to see the best in myself.
I choose to see the best in others.

EVENING AFFIRMATIONS

I honor and respect my body by taking good care of it.
I always have time for self-love and self-care.

DAY 17

MORNING AFFIRMATIONS

My life and my presence is a blessing to others.
I am free to create and live the life of my dreams.

EVENING AFFIRMATIONS

My smile is so bright that it lights up every room I walk into.
It is easy for me to be playful and lighthearted.

DAY 18

MORNING AFFIRMATIONS

I'm open to receiving infinite abundance and blessings.
I attract the best opportunities every step of the way.

EVENING AFFIRMATIONS

I embrace and honor my needs, desires, and wants.
All my needs, desires, and wants are getting easily fulfilled.

DAY 19

MORNING AFFIRMATIONS

I enjoy seeing the best in others.
Other people see the best in me wherever I go.

EVENING AFFIRMATIONS

I am deeply loved and appreciated by everyone in my life.
My body and my being is radiating infinite unconditional love.

DAY 20

MORNING AFFIRMATIONS

I am exactly where I should be at this very moment.
Everything is working out perfectly for me.

EVENING AFFIRMATIONS

I am whole and complete exactly the way I am.
Other people love and honor me exactly the way I am.

DAY 21

MORNING AFFIRMATIONS

I have the power to create whatever I desire.
My destiny is in my hands.

EVENING AFFIRMATIONS

I am unique and very special.
I am treated like royalty wherever I go.

DAY 22

MORNING AFFIRMATIONS

I smile and laugh easily.
My heart is filled with joy and happiness.

EVENING AFFIRMATIONS

I am open to new experiences and adventures.
I trust that I am always at the perfect place at the perfect time.

DAY 23

MORNING AFFIRMATIONS

I treat myself with respect.
Everyone in my life treats me with respect.

EVENING AFFIRMATIONS

I have complete faith in myself.
I can handle any situation with grace, gratitude, and joy.

DAY 24

MORNING AFFIRMATIONS

I am courageous and hardworking.
Other people value my knowledge, skills, and hard work.

EVENING AFFIRMATIONS

I have infinite potential for greatness.
I have come into this world to do extraordinary things.

DAY 25

MORNING AFFIRMATIONS

I enjoy eating healthy and nutritious food.
I treat healthy food as fuel for my body and mind.

EVENING AFFIRMATIONS

My body and my mind are sacred.
I am an infinite divine being.

DAY 26

MORNING AFFIRMATIONS

I have the most supportive family and friends.
Other people always wish the best for me.

EVENING AFFIRMATIONS

I am here to own my divinity and awesomeness.
I am fully embracing the beauty of my soul.

DAY 27

MORNING AFFIRMATIONS

I am the most amazing person in the whole world.
It is easy for me to be kind and empathetic towards others.

EVENING AFFIRMATIONS

My presence inspires others to be their best self.
I am a very forgiving and loving person.

DAY 28

MORNING AFFIRMATIONS

I always treat myself with love and compassion.
I am my own Source for love and abundance.

EVENING AFFIRMATIONS

All my dreams are rapidly manifesting in my reality.
I am already living the life of my dreams.

DAY 29

MORNING AFFIRMATIONS

I appreciate the gift of life.
Every moment that I am alive is truly a blessing.

EVENING AFFIRMATIONS

I am capable of doing incredible things.
I am helping create a better world through my contributions.

DAY 30

MORNING AFFIRMATIONS

Setting healthy boundaries comes easily and naturally to me.
I feel I am a truly amazing person.

EVENING AFFIRMATIONS

I am always excited about life.
I know and trust that everything is happening for my highest good.

DAY 31

MORNING AFFIRMATIONS

I am beaming with self-confidence.
I have the power to turn any challenge into a victory.

EVENING AFFIRMATIONS

I am constantly growing and expanding my horizons.
I am the most confident person in the room.

DAY 32

MORNING AFFIRMATIONS

I can do anything I set my mind to.
All things are possible for me.

EVENING AFFIRMATIONS

I love who I am.
I love who I am becoming.

DAY 33

MORNING AFFIRMATIONS

My life is perfect.
I have everything I can wish for and more.

EVENING AFFIRMATIONS

I recognize and embrace the fact that my body is the temple of my soul.
Taking care of my body and soul is so much fun.

DAY 34

MORNING AFFIRMATIONS

I believe in myself.
I am an achiever. I go after what I want and I always get it.

EVENING AFFIRMATIONS

I relentlessly pursue my goals and my dreams.
The Universe bends over backwards to give me what I want.

DAY 35

MORNING AFFIRMATIONS

My life is profoundly rewarding and fulfilling.
I am comfortable being myself.

EVENING AFFIRMATIONS

I have a kind and caring heart.
I am good to everyone in my life including myself.

DAY 36

MORNING AFFIRMATIONS

I deserve to be loved and cherished.
I graciously receive the blessings that come to me through others.

EVENING AFFIRMATIONS

I am sensitive to my body's needs.
I treat my body with love and kindness.

DAY 37

MORNING AFFIRMATIONS

I expect the best out of life and out of myself.
I trust that there is infinite abundance in the world for everyone.

EVENING AFFIRMATIONS

Other people love being around me.
I spread joy wherever I go.

DAY 38

MORNING AFFIRMATIONS

I am worthy of all the love and kindness I receive from others.
My life is truly abundant in every way possible.

EVENING AFFIRMATIONS

I am falling more and more in love with myself every day.
I appreciate myself for who I am.

DAY 39

MORNING AFFIRMATIONS

I am kind and generous.
I always have time for the things that I love doing.

EVENING AFFIRMATIONS

My birth is a blessing to this world.
The world is a better place because I am here.

DAY 40

MORNING AFFIRMATIONS

I choose to be my best self every day.
I am an amazing human being.

EVENING AFFIRMATIONS

The source of my love and joy is within me.
I am whole. I am complete.

DAY 41

MORNING AFFIRMATIONS

Everything that I need at this moment is already mine.
I have the power to overcome any challenge.

EVENING AFFIRMATIONS

I am an extremely strong person.
I keep getting stronger and stronger with every passing day.

DAY 42

MORNING AFFIRMATIONS

The only person whose opinion truly matters is me.
I am the only one I have to impress.

EVENING AFFIRMATIONS

I am my own competition.
I am a success because every single day I become an even better person
than who I was yesterday.

DAY 43

MORNING AFFIRMATIONS

I am an eternal optimist.
I always hope for the very best in every situation.

EVENING AFFIRMATIONS

I trust that with every step in the right direction, I am getting closer and
closer to my goals.
I take pride in everything I do.

DAY 44

MORNING AFFIRMATIONS

I am in love with myself.
I rely only on myself for unconditional love and support.

EVENING AFFIRMATIONS

I allow myself to feel all my emotions.
I honor and cherish all my emotions.

DAY 45

MORNING AFFIRMATIONS

I create my own path.
I am outstanding at everything I do.

EVENING AFFIRMATIONS

With every passing day, my life is becoming more beautiful.
I am evolving into the highest version of myself.

DAY 46

MORNING AFFIRMATIONS

I am valuable and worthy exactly the way I am.
I choose to see and connect with the perfection in myself.

EVENING AFFIRMATIONS

I am a positive and happy person.
I deserve joy, success, and happiness.

DAY 47

MORNING AFFIRMATIONS

I have the power to create the best future for myself.
I am in charge of my life and my destiny.

EVENING AFFIRMATIONS

Everything always works out favourably for me.
I smile with ease because I am always so happy.

DAY 48

MORNING AFFIRMATIONS

I accept compliments gracefully.
It is easy for me to say 'no' to anything that doesn't feel right to my heart.

EVENING AFFIRMATIONS

I am living a balanced and harmonious life.
I am allowing love and joy to flow to me.

DAY 49

MORNING AFFIRMATIONS

It is easy for me to love wholeheartedly and completely.
I know that my inner reality creates my outer experiences.

EVENING AFFIRMATIONS

I choose to think only happy thoughts.
I imagine only good things happening to me.

DAY 50

MORNING AFFIRMATIONS

I know I can have anything I truly want.
The Universe is limitless. My potential to experience abundance is
infinite.

EVENING AFFIRMATIONS

There are infinite opportunities for growth.
Every day, I am growing and becoming the best version of myself.

DAY 51

MORNING AFFIRMATIONS

Today, I will do my best at every task I perform.
I seek progress and constant self-improvement.

EVENING AFFIRMATIONS

I love all my flaws and imperfections.
I am a beautiful person inside and out.

DAY 52

MORNING AFFIRMATIONS

I have the power to deal with whatever may come my way.
It is easy for me to focus on the blessing in every situation.

EVENING AFFIRMATIONS

I am fit, strong, and healthy.
I am capable of doing amazing things.

DAY 53

MORNING AFFIRMATIONS

I accept myself fully and completely.
I am at peace with myself and my life.

EVENING AFFIRMATIONS

Good health comes to me easily and effortlessly.
I am grateful to my body through which I live and enjoy life.

DAY 54

MORNING AFFIRMATIONS

I am always energetic and enthusiastic.
I love living life to the fullest.

EVENING AFFIRMATIONS

I think only what I want to experience in my physical reality.
I have mastered my mind and my emotions.

DAY 55

MORNING AFFIRMATIONS

I love nurturing my body with healthy food.
For me, eating healthy food is pleasurable and enjoyable.

EVENING AFFIRMATIONS

I am proud of my body.
My body is truly amazing and perfect.

DAY 56

MORNING AFFIRMATIONS

I'm excited to be alive and enjoying life.
I trust that all my dreams have manifested in my material reality.

EVENING AFFIRMATIONS

My body deserves to be treated with love and respect.
I enjoy giving adequate rest to my body.

DAY 57

MORNING AFFIRMATIONS

My life is a gift.
I love my life and all the blessings I have received in it.

EVENING AFFIRMATIONS

I am at my perfect weight and size.
My body is perfect for me.

DAY 58

MORNING AFFIRMATIONS

My body is a priceless gift.
I admire and love my body.

EVENING AFFIRMATIONS

I am always glowing with good health and happiness.
My happiness and positivity is infectious to others.

DAY 59

MORNING AFFIRMATIONS

It is easy for me to always think happy and positive thoughts.
I'm my own greatest cheerleader.

EVENING AFFIRMATIONS

I enjoy my own company whenever I am alone.
I value and cherish my relationship with myself.

DAY 60

MORNING AFFIRMATIONS

What a beautiful day it is to be alive and happy!
I wake up every morning with excitement and go to bed with
satisfaction.

EVENING AFFIRMATIONS

Every day of my life is filled with happiness and joy.
I am a winner!

DAY 61

MORNING AFFIRMATIONS

I always see the glass half-full.
I already am the person I have always wanted to be.

EVENING AFFIRMATIONS

It is easy for me to be gentle and kind to myself.
I am bold, confident, and amazing.

DAY 62

MORNING AFFIRMATIONS

I am perfection personified.
I receive love and kindness wherever I go.

EVENING AFFIRMATIONS

Today, I am choosing to count all my blessings.
I have so much to be thankful for.

DAY 63

MORNING AFFIRMATIONS

I love how my life keeps getting better and better.
My life is truly full and abundant.

EVENING AFFIRMATIONS

It is easy for me to do my best under all circumstances.
Everyone around me is loving and supportive towards me.

DAY 64

MORNING AFFIRMATIONS

I choose to believe in myself no matter what anyone else says.
I have a strong zest for life. I'm always enjoying myself.

EVENING AFFIRMATIONS

I'm a high-value woman/man.
I deserve to be treated like royalty.

DAY 65

MORNING AFFIRMATIONS

My beautiful soul shines brightly like a diamond.
Other people see and acknowledge how amazing I am!

EVENING AFFIRMATIONS

I celebrate every moment of life.
I'm irresistible and incredibly charming.

DAY 66

MORNING AFFIRMATIONS

I'm so happy that all my dreams are coming true!
It's amazing how nice everyone everywhere always is to me.

EVENING AFFIRMATIONS

I honor my personal boundaries.
I say no to all that doesn't feel right to me.

DAY 67

MORNING AFFIRMATIONS

I have the courage to take a stand for myself under all circumstances.
I am happy that everything is working out so wonderfully for me.

EVENING AFFIRMATIONS

Other people find me inspiring and admirable.
I am a positive example for everyone around me.

DAY 68

MORNING AFFIRMATIONS

I look absolutely stunning.
People admire my inner and outer beauty wherever I go.

EVENING AFFIRMATIONS

Everyone always wants the best for me.
I bring out the best in others.

DAY 69

MORNING AFFIRMATIONS

I enjoy exercising because it is an opportunity for me to take care of my
body.
I enjoy staying active throughout the day.

EVENING AFFIRMATIONS

I am fully relaxed and at peace.
I sleep peacefully every night.

DAY 70

MORNING AFFIRMATIONS

I am always feeling fresh and energetic.
I am so blessed and joyful.

EVENING AFFIRMATIONS

I live my life by my own rules.
I always do what feels right to my heart.

DAY 71

MORNING AFFIRMATIONS

My heart is beating with profound unconditional love.
I listen to and trust my intuition.

EVENING AFFIRMATIONS

I enjoy being authentic and honest.
I always choose my inner peace under all circumstances.

DAY 72

MORNING AFFIRMATIONS

I am healed. I am whole.
I am an incredibly valuable person.

EVENING AFFIRMATIONS

I am fierce, authentic, and genuine.
Other people acknowledge and connect with my best qualities.

DAY 73

MORNING AFFIRMATIONS

I am committed to constant self-improvement.
The only one I compete with is the person I see in the mirror every day.

EVENING AFFIRMATIONS

I give enough rest to my body and mind every day.
I trust that what is meant for me would come to me when the timing is right.

DAY 74

MORNING AFFIRMATIONS

I speak with kindness and thoughtfulness.
I hear only good and positive words.

EVENING AFFIRMATIONS

I acknowledge and accept all my emotions as they come and go.
I honor my mind, my emotions, and my feelings.

DAY 75

MORNING AFFIRMATIONS

I have the skills and the talent to achieve my goals.
Everything always works out in my favor.

EVENING AFFIRMATIONS

I have outgrown my past.
I am the finest and best version of myself today.

DAY 76

MORNING AFFIRMATIONS

I have the confidence to face every life situation.
I enjoy being good and doing good.

EVENING AFFIRMATIONS

I am here to change the world for the better.
I understand my value and self-worth.

DAY 77

MORNING AFFIRMATIONS

I'm a strong and powerful woman/man.
I know that I am destined for greatness and success.

EVENING AFFIRMATIONS

I value my time and energy.
I am at peace knowing that I am doing my very best.

DAY 78

MORNING AFFIRMATIONS

I wish everyone well.
I'm always surrounded by well wishers.

EVENING AFFIRMATIONS

I have a beautiful and pure heart.
For me, every day is a good day.

DAY 79

MORNING AFFIRMATIONS

The light in my heart illuminates the lives of everyone around me.
I bring joy, happiness, and smiles to everyone.

EVENING AFFIRMATIONS

I always find a way to do what I love.
For me, everything is possible.

DAY 80

MORNING AFFIRMATIONS

I feel gratitude in my heart every moment of the day.
I always treat myself respectfully and honorably.

EVENING AFFIRMATIONS

I choose to focus on the bright side of things.
I believe in infinite hope and positivity.

DAY 81

MORNING AFFIRMATIONS

I believe in magic and miracles.
The Universe is fulfilling all my heart's desires.

EVENING AFFIRMATIONS

I think big. I dream big.
Big wonderful things happen to me all the time.

DAY 82

MORNING AFFIRMATIONS

I am a glorious being with a magnificent heart.
I am open and ready to receive all the blessings the Universe is bringing
to me right now.

EVENING AFFIRMATIONS

My life is unfolding according to a perfect divine plan.
I have the courage to manifest and fulfil all my dreams.

DAY 83

MORNING AFFIRMATIONS

I am always learning, improving, and growing.
I can only become stronger and more amazing with every passing day.

EVENING AFFIRMATIONS

Every day of my life is the best day of my life.
I'm an absolutely incredible person who deserves only the very best that
life has to offer.

DAY 84

MORNING AFFIRMATIONS

I love how beautiful/handsome I am.
My face shines with the glow of happiness and positivity.

EVENING AFFIRMATIONS

I am free to be truly myself.
I embrace myself completely with all my perfections and imperfections.

DAY 85

MORNING AFFIRMATIONS

I celebrate myself every day.
I reward myself for all the things I do right.

EVENING AFFIRMATIONS

I love being my own best friend.
The only person whose love, care, and acceptance I need is me.

DAY 86

MORNING AFFIRMATIONS

I am comfortable expressing my thoughts and ideas to others.
I am fearless, bold, and confident.

EVENING AFFIRMATIONS

I can walk into any room and completely own the room.
It is amazing how much other people love and admire me!

DAY 87

MORNING AFFIRMATIONS

I am always receiving pleasant and wonderful surprises.
I am the most optimistic and happiest person I know.

EVENING AFFIRMATIONS

I have very strong boundaries.
I evoke respect and reverence in others.

DAY 88

MORNING AFFIRMATIONS

I love everything about myself and my life.
I accept, acknowledge, and appreciate the beauty of my soul.

EVENING AFFIRMATIONS

I am grateful to be living my dream life.
I always have more abundance than I need and desire.

DAY 89

MORNING AFFIRMATIONS

I am a perfect divine being who deserves all the happiness in the world.
I am a creative and ambitious person. I succeed at everything I do.

EVENING AFFIRMATIONS

I am very comfortable in my own skin.
I am the best me there can ever be.

DAY 90

MORNING AFFIRMATIONS

People admire how happy and positive I always am.
My work and contributions make the world a better place.

EVENING AFFIRMATIONS

I love living my life with grace and gratitude.
I appreciate myself for all the good that I do.

DAY 91

MORNING AFFIRMATIONS

I enjoy receiving compliments.
I accept compliments with gratitude and ease.

EVENING AFFIRMATIONS

I am a person with high moral standards.
I always conduct myself with dignity and self-respect.

DAY 92

MORNING AFFIRMATIONS

Today, I am choosing to focus on all the opportunities that surround me.
I am living my dream life every single day.

EVENING AFFIRMATIONS

I have the capability to handle anything and everything.
I keep growing and evolving with every challenge that I overcome.

DAY 93

MORNING AFFIRMATIONS

My mind has unlimited power to attract whatever I desire.
The world is truly my oyster. If I can dream it, I can have it.

EVENING AFFIRMATIONS

I am fond of myself.
I am content being myself.

DAY 94

MORNING AFFIRMATIONS

I am a high achiever.
My confidence and faith in myself keeps growing every day.

EVENING AFFIRMATIONS

I accept and honor my past exactly the way it is.
I trust that my future is bright and beautiful.

DAY 95

MORNING AFFIRMATIONS

There is so much that I love about myself.
The more I love myself, the easier it is for me to love others.

EVENING AFFIRMATIONS

I embrace my individuality and uniqueness.
I accept and honor my life path.

DAY 96

MORNING AFFIRMATIONS

I relish every moment of being alive.
I am living every moment of life with an open heart.

EVENING AFFIRMATIONS

I trust that my future is going to be exactly how I want it to be.
I trust that right at this very moment, all my dreams are coming true.

DAY 97

My body is a perfect work of art.
I admire and respect my body for all that it does for me.

EVENING AFFIRMATIONS

I am exactly who I need to be at this very moment.
I accept myself and my life exactly the way it is right now.

DAY 98

MORNING AFFIRMATIONS

I dare to dream big.
I have the courage and the passion to pursue my dreams with relentless
commitment.

EVENING AFFIRMATIONS

I hope to always get the very best out of life.
The Universe provides for me under all circumstances.

DAY 99

MORNING AFFIRMATIONS

I am kind and loving towards my body.
I choose to see my life as a beautiful gift.

EVENING AFFIRMATIONS

Love is the very essence of my being.
It is very easy for me to love myself and others unconditionally.

DAY 100

MORNING AFFIRMATIONS

I find joy in every moment.
I perform all my duties and tasks with great love.

EVENING AFFIRMATIONS

I am a generous and compassionate person.
I enjoy helping others.

DAY 101

MORNING AFFIRMATIONS

All my big and small dreams are supported by the Universe.
Luck always favors me.

EVENING AFFIRMATIONS

I am forgiving myself for all the mistakes I have ever made.
I have the ability to do what is good and what is right.

DAY 102

MORNING AFFIRMATIONS

I am proud of all my achievements.
Achieving my goals is fun and exciting.

EVENING AFFIRMATIONS

I deserve an amazing life.
My mind is always buzzing with amazing ideas.

DAY 103

MORNING AFFIRMATIONS

I trust my vision and plan for life.
I have full faith in my ability to achieve all my goals.

EVENING AFFIRMATIONS

I am grounded in self-love.
In this moment, everything is exactly the way it should be.

DAY 104

MORNING AFFIRMATIONS

I am bigger than all my thoughts.
I am an infinite soul experiencing infinite abundance.

EVENING AFFIRMATIONS

Self-love comes easily and naturally to me.
I am self-sufficient and perfectly capable of meeting all my needs.

DAY 105

MORNING AFFIRMATIONS

The Universe is always on my side.
I always get what is best for me in the moment.

EVENING AFFIRMATIONS

I am an extraordinary person with an extraordinary life.
Greatness is in my DNA.

DAY 106

MORNING AFFIRMATIONS

I am happy and prosperous.
I am confident that victory is my birthright.

EVENING AFFIRMATIONS

At this moment, I am exactly who I need to be.
I am the most charismatic and charming person I know.

DAY 107

MORNING AFFIRMATIONS

I have a magnetic personality.
Other people are attracted to me because I am absolutely awesome.

EVENING AFFIRMATIONS

I deserve all the good that is happening to me.
I am blessed beyond measure.

DAY 108

MORNING AFFIRMATIONS

I trust the wisdom of my soul – the voice of my intuition.
I feel I am an amazing person – my opinion is all that matters.

EVENING AFFIRMATIONS

I have lived another perfect day in this beautiful world.
I have everything I need to live a fulfilling and happy life.

DAY 109

MORNING AFFIRMATIONS

I have a captivating personality.
People truly enjoy my company and love having me around.

EVENING AFFIRMATIONS

I am always grounded and centered in inner peace.
I am a high performer constantly breaking my personal records.

DAY 110

MORNING AFFIRMATIONS

I deserve compliments and praise.
I enjoy receiving admiration from others.

EVENING AFFIRMATIONS

I am doing outstandingly well in life.
My life is the kind of things that dreams are made of.

DAY 111

MORNING AFFIRMATIONS

I take full responsibility for everything that is happening in my life.
It is my responsibility to turn all my dreams into reality.

EVENING AFFIRMATIONS

My life is overflowing with grace, positivity, and abundance.
I am grateful to be living such a blessed and beautiful life.

DAY 112

MORNING AFFIRMATIONS

I am very good at taking care of myself.
I cherish and adore myself.

EVENING AFFIRMATIONS

I deserve all the appreciation that I receive.
I am a genuine and authentic person that other people look up to.

DAY 113

MORNING AFFIRMATIONS

All my dreams are within my reach.
I can have, be, and do anything I set my mind to.

EVENING AFFIRMATIONS

Every day, I am becoming more and more aware of how amazing I am.
Every day, I attract miracles and blessings into my life.

DAY 114

MORNING AFFIRMATIONS

I deserve to live a wonderful blessed life.
I persevere in the pursuit of my dreams.

EVENING AFFIRMATIONS

My voice and my opinions are important.
Other people honor and respect my opinions.

DAY 115

MORNING AFFIRMATIONS

I am a brave and courageous person.
I am living my best life.

EVENING AFFIRMATIONS

I am empowered by my profound self-love.
I am invincible.

DAY 116

MORNING AFFIRMATIONS

I am confident and assertive.
I have the courage to take a stand for everything that I believe in.

EVENING AFFIRMATIONS

I am a person with values and principles.
I deserve to live a rich and blessed life.

DAY 117

MORNING AFFIRMATIONS

I am the only one who is responsible for my happiness.
I am a cheerful and happy person.

EVENING AFFIRMATIONS

I like being kind and generous towards myself.
I attract kindness and generosity from others.

DAY 118

MORNING AFFIRMATIONS

Today is a wonderful and positive day.
Every situation is unfolding in my favor.

EVENING AFFIRMATIONS

I accept and acknowledge all the blessings that surround me at this very
moment.
I enjoy the process of working towards my goals.

DAY 119

MORNING AFFIRMATIONS

I always make my physical, mental, emotional, and spiritual health a
priority.
I have an extremely strong body and mind.

EVENING AFFIRMATIONS

All my decisions are aligned with my highest good.
I am a powerful and successful person in every area of life.

DAY 120

MORNING AFFIRMATIONS

I acknowledge and accept all my fears.
I'm letting go of all my fears right now. From now on, I have the courage
to do whatever I must do.

EVENING AFFIRMATIONS

I always claim victory as my birthright.
I have mastered the art of living in the present and always imagining the
best for the future.

DAY 121

MORNING AFFIRMATIONS

It is easy for me to respect my own boundaries.
Others must always treat me with great respect.

EVENING AFFIRMATIONS

I feel I am a beautiful and lovable person.
Other people feel honoured and privileged to be around me.

DAY 122

MORNING AFFIRMATIONS

I am strong and resilient.
I count my blessings and emerge victorious in every situation.

EVENING AFFIRMATIONS

I have control over my mind and my emotions.
I choose to think and feel only those thoughts and emotions that serve
my highest good.

DAY 123

MORNING AFFIRMATIONS

I am sending deep unconditional love to all my doubts and fears.
All my fears and doubts have transformed into pure love and peace.

EVENING AFFIRMATIONS

I am giving myself permission to say no to anything that doesn't feel
right.
I have the power and the ability to take well-informed decisions in all
situations.

DAY 124

MORNING AFFIRMATIONS

I choose my dignity and self-respect.
I am committed to making myself a priority.

EVENING AFFIRMATIONS

Today I am embracing all the love that is flowing towards me from all sources.
All my daily actions and habits are aligned with my soul's purpose.

DAY 125

MORNING AFFIRMATIONS

Today is a perfect day to be truly myself.
I am beaming with positivity, love, and confidence.

EVENING AFFIRMATIONS

I am a deeply compassionate and loving person.
I have a kind, warm, and loving heart.

DAY 126

MORNING AFFIRMATIONS

I love myself for who I truly am.
There is no one like me.

EVENING AFFIRMATIONS

I am capable of greatness and extraordinary things.
I am choosing to be my best and give my best today.

DAY 127

MORNING AFFIRMATIONS

I am truly proud of who I am.
There never was, isn't, and never will be another me.

EVENING AFFIRMATIONS

I am capable of living a truly outstanding life.
My best self shines through in every situation.

DAY 128

MORNING AFFIRMATIONS

I attract grace, love, beauty, and blessings.
My life is full of happiness, love, and laughter.

EVENING AFFIRMATIONS

The Universe always takes care of me.
It is safe, comfortable, and easy for me to relax and let go.

DAY 129

MORNING AFFIRMATIONS

I am a positive influence on everyone around me.
People feel inspired and uplifted in my presence.

EVENING AFFIRMATIONS

I know how to enjoy life to the fullest.
I have the ability to turn any situation into a favorable one for me.

DAY 130

MORNING AFFIRMATIONS

I receive royal treatment wherever I go.
I'm the type of person everyone admires.

EVENING AFFIRMATIONS

My capacity for giving and receiving love is infinite.
I am infinitely abundant in every way possible.

DAY 131

MORNING AFFIRMATIONS

I am surrounded by happy and positive people.
I love how encouraging everyone in my life is towards me.

EVENING AFFIRMATIONS

I have mastered the art of taking inspired action every day.
My intuition guides me every step of the way.

DAY 132

MORNING AFFIRMATIONS

It is easy for me to get along with others.
I am very good at making other people feel comfortable and safe.

EVENING AFFIRMATIONS

I really enjoy my alone time.
I like to take the time to nurture and nourish myself.

DAY 133

MORNING AFFIRMATIONS

I am the writer and director of my life.
The movie of my life is always going to play out the way I want it to be.

EVENING AFFIRMATIONS

I am proud of all my accomplishments.
Every challenge that I face makes me stronger and wiser.

DAY 134

MORNING AFFIRMATIONS

All my doubts and fears are transforming into self-confidence.
I have full faith in my ability to manifest my perfect life.

EVENING AFFIRMATIONS

I am patient, understanding, and kind.
I include myself in my circle of compassion.

DAY 135

MORNING AFFIRMATIONS

It is easy for me to see what is best for me in any situation.
I always choose to act with integrity and self-respect.

EVENING AFFIRMATIONS

I use the power of my imagination to visualize only what I truly want.
I am attracting infinite blessings into my life.

DAY 136

MORNING AFFIRMATIONS

Other people recognize and connect with the beauty of my soul.
I am brilliant and outstanding in every way.

EVENING AFFIRMATIONS

All my thoughts are aligned with my heart's truest desires.
I have completely mastered my thoughts and my mind.

DAY 137

MORNING AFFIRMATIONS

I have a positive and uplifting energy field.
Anyone who comes near me feels positively recharged and uplifted.

EVENING AFFIRMATIONS

I trust that I can achieve any goal I set for myself.
Whatever I want comes to me easily and effortlessly.

DAY 138

MORNING AFFIRMATIONS

It is amazing how much people love me.
I totally deserve the love I receive from others.

EVENING AFFIRMATIONS

I have the power to manifest anything I need or want into my reality.
I trust the Universe is bringing me whatever is best for me in perfect
divine timing.

DAY 139

MORNING AFFIRMATIONS

I accept and love all aspects of my personality.
I am choosing to see the best in me and in others.

EVENING AFFIRMATIONS

The source of my love and joy lies within my own heart.
Self-care and self-love are major priorities for me.

DAY 140

MORNING AFFIRMATIONS

All the tools I need for success are already at my disposal.
I know how to recognize and make the most out of any opportunity that
comes my way.

EVENING AFFIRMATIONS

I have released my past completely.
I am ready for an amazing present and future.

DAY 141

MORNING AFFIRMATIONS

I am a very pleasant and easy person to be around.
Everyone always has the best things to say about me.

EVENING AFFIRMATIONS

I am a truly wonderful and valuable person.
Everyone who is close to me believes that I am a blessing in their life.

DAY 142

MORNING AFFIRMATIONS

Every day is an opportunity to start a new life.
I am recognizing and honoring all the blessings that I currently have in my life.

EVENING AFFIRMATIONS

I am willing to release anything that is no longer working for me.
I accept praise and compliments with ease.

DAY 143

MORNING AFFIRMATIONS

Today I am giving myself permission to be truly myself.
It is easy for me to maintain balance and harmony in my life.

EVENING AFFIRMATIONS

I have the power to make whatever changes I desire in myself and in my life.
I am embracing peace, happiness, and joy.

DAY 144

MORNING AFFIRMATIONS

Self-love is the highest form of love.
I choose to love myself unconditionally under all circumstances.

EVENING AFFIRMATIONS

I am an incredibly beautiful person.
I am always confident, self-assured, and happy.

DAY 145

MORNING AFFIRMATIONS

I am experiencing boundless infinite joy.
By accepting the constantly changing nature of things, I am always
learning and growing.

EVENING AFFIRMATIONS

I am always surrounded by wonderful people who want the best for me.
People always treat me with great generosity and consideration.

DAY 146

MORNING AFFIRMATIONS

I trust that there are endless opportunities for success and happiness.
If anything doesn't work out, it is because the Universe has something
better for me.

EVENING AFFIRMATIONS

I appreciate and reward myself for everything I do well.
Self-love and self-respect come easily to me.

DAY 147

MORNING AFFIRMATIONS

I am ready for a fresh start.
I trust that everything is working in my favor.

EVENING AFFIRMATIONS

The Universe supports all my goals.
My life is filled with exciting opportunities.

DAY 148

MORNING AFFIRMATIONS

I have a growth mindset.
It is easy for me to focus on what is good and positive in every situation.

EVENING AFFIRMATIONS

I treat my body as the temple of my soul.
I am sensitive to the needs of my body.

DAY 149

MORNING AFFIRMATIONS

I prioritize my health and well-being.
I choose to make myself my highest priority.

EVENING AFFIRMATIONS

My heart always tells me the truth.
I am choosing to heed the infinite wisdom of my heart.

DAY 150

MORNING AFFIRMATIONS

I have the power and the ability to do absolutely incredible things.
I always take the best decision in every situation.

EVENING AFFIRMATIONS

My self-confidence keeps growing every day.
Others find me irresistibly charming.

DAY 151

MORNING AFFIRMATIONS

I am a magnet for positivity and good things.
I have the power to transform my life.

EVENING AFFIRMATIONS

All my thoughts, ideas, and plans are leading me to success.
Every day I keep becoming finer than the finest version of myself.

DAY 152

MORNING AFFIRMATIONS

I start every day feeling confident, happy, and empowered.
I attract success wherever I go.

EVENING AFFIRMATIONS

I exude self-confidence.
I have the courage to follow through on all my decisions.

DAY 153

MORNING AFFIRMATIONS

The power of the entire infinite Universe is within me.
Every step I take brings me closer and closer to success.

EVENING AFFIRMATIONS

I am the most optimistic and positive person I know.
I feel extremely happy, whole, and complete.

DAY 154

MORNING AFFIRMATIONS

I start every day feeling energetic and motivated.
Every morning, I jump out of bed feeling excited and enthusiastic.

EVENING AFFIRMATIONS

My presence makes the world a better place.
I constantly keep exceeding my own expectations.

DAY 155

MORNING AFFIRMATIONS

I know that today is going to be a phenomenal day.
It is amazing how I always manage to be at the right place at the right time!

EVENING AFFIRMATIONS

I think happy and positive thoughts.
I allow myself to be led by my dreams.

DAY 156

MORNING AFFIRMATIONS

I have learned from my past and I have released it completely.
I am driven by my dreams for the future and my commitment to the present.

EVENING AFFIRMATIONS

Every obstacle inspires me to level up my game.
Every day, I keep getting stronger and smarter.

DAY 157

MORNING AFFIRMATIONS

I am deeply grateful for every single thing I have in my life.
I am free to be whoever I wish to be.

EVENING AFFIRMATIONS

I am a very independent and self-sufficient person.
I rely on myself for fulfilling all my needs.

DAY 158

MORNING AFFIRMATIONS

Today is going to be a positive and productive day.
I seek to be a blessing in other people's lives.

EVENING AFFIRMATIONS

I am witty and intelligent.
My brain is extremely sharp.

DAY 159

MORNING AFFIRMATIONS

I keep getting happier and healthier every day.
I am razor focused on my goals.

EVENING AFFIRMATIONS

I know I am a good person.
Others recognize the goodness of my heart and soul.

DAY 160

MORNING AFFIRMATIONS

I have forgiven my past.
I am fully embracing this present moment.

EVENING AFFIRMATIONS

My heart has completely healed.
My heart is full of love, dreams, and hope.

DAY 161

MORNING AFFIRMATIONS

All my thoughts are constructive and positive.
I hope for the best in every situation.

EVENING AFFIRMATIONS

I am obsessed with growth and personal transformation.
I make the most of every single day of my life.

DAY 162

MORNING AFFIRMATIONS

I am strong enough to emerge victorious in every situation.
I am an exceptionally beautiful person.

EVENING AFFIRMATIONS

My only competition is with myself.
I am committed to being better than who I was yesterday.

DAY 163

MORNING AFFIRMATIONS

I am proud of the person that I am right now.
I am perfect in every possible way.

EVENING AFFIRMATIONS

I finish every important task I undertake.
I have the wisdom to release and let go of the things that don't really matter.

DAY 164

MORNING AFFIRMATIONS

I set clear goals that I pursue with complete dedication.
Today, I am choosing to be happy.

EVENING AFFIRMATIONS

Sleep comes to me easily and effortlessly.
I go to bed every night feeling content and satisfied that I did the best I could throughout the day.

DAY 165

MORNING AFFIRMATIONS

I am excited for another beautiful and blissful day.
I am always happy.

EVENING AFFIRMATIONS

I adapt well to all situations in life.
I understand that every situation in life is giving me a chance to grow and become even more awesome.

DAY 166

MORNING AFFIRMATIONS

I am excited to kickstart another amazing day on such a positive note.
I always stay happy and positive.

EVENING AFFIRMATIONS

I am stronger and smarter than all my fears.
I have the power to rise above all adversity and challenges.

DAY 167

MORNING AFFIRMATIONS

I am a huge success at everything I do.
I give myself permission to be totally awesome.

EVENING AFFIRMATIONS

I enjoy going to bed on time and waking up refreshed.
I look forward to waking up refreshed and rejuvenated after a good
night's sleep.

DAY 168

MORNING AFFIRMATIONS

I have control over my emotions.
I choose happy and positive emotions.

EVENING AFFIRMATIONS

I can achieve everything I desire.
I am stronger and smarter than I realize.

DAY 169

MORNING AFFIRMATIONS

I embrace change with ease and excitement.
I enjoy exploring and living up to my full potential.

EVENING AFFIRMATIONS

I am grateful for every experience I have had in this life.
I am who I am because of every single thing I have experienced and lived
through.

DAY 170

MORNING AFFIRMATIONS

I keep trying until I succeed.
Success is my only choice.

EVENING AFFIRMATIONS

It is safe for me to express my emotions.
I already have everything that I can possibly need to succeed.

DAY 171

MORNING AFFIRMATIONS

I learn and grow from every setback.
I am committed to learning something new every day.

EVENING AFFIRMATIONS

I am choosing to embrace all my flaws and imperfections.
I may not be perfect but there is always going to be just one 'ME.'

DAY 172

MORNING AFFIRMATIONS

I deserve to feel amazing about myself.
I absolutely love my reflection in the mirror.

EVENING AFFIRMATIONS

Other people love spending time with me.
I am an absolute delight to be with.

DAY 173

MORNING AFFIRMATIONS

Today is my chance to shine again and be awesome.
I enjoy looking at my reflection in the mirror.

EVENING AFFIRMATIONS

I am a wonderful person who deserves to be treated with respect.
I have the ability to charm anyone I like.

DAY 174

MORNING AFFIRMATIONS

I feel confident and self-assured in every situation.
I trust my intuition enough to take risks whenever I am guided to do so.

EVENING AFFIRMATIONS

I am choosing to be around people whose company I truly enjoy.
I trust that the future is bright and favorable for me.

DAY 175

MORNING AFFIRMATIONS

I have released all my mental blocks.
I am ready for infinite abundance.

EVENING AFFIRMATIONS

After every setback, I come back stronger and even more determined.
Success is my only option.

DAY 176

MORNING AFFIRMATIONS

Every day brings with it new possibilities and opportunities.
All my daily choices and actions are aligned with my goals.

EVENING AFFIRMATIONS

I am an excellent decision maker.
I am excited about the future.

DAY 177

MORNING AFFIRMATIONS

I am committed to improving myself in every possible way.
Self-improvement is my greatest passion and a natural way of life.

EVENING AFFIRMATIONS

My feelings and emotions are important.
Other people respect my feelings and emotions.

DAY 178

MORNING AFFIRMATIONS

I love the person that I am.
My enthusiasm and zest for life is infectious.

EVENING AFFIRMATIONS

I have mastered the art of getting along with others.
I make friends wherever I go.

DAY 179

MORNING AFFIRMATIONS

I enjoy trying new things.
I adapt to change easily and enthusiastically.

EVENING AFFIRMATIONS

I am grateful for the amazing person that I am.
I am choosing to focus on that which I can control and change.

DAY 180

MORNING AFFIRMATIONS

I am comfortable asking for help whenever I need it.
Other people are always eager to help me.

EVENING AFFIRMATIONS

My mind is always overflowing with creative ideas.
I choose to see the best in every situation.

DAY 181

MORNING AFFIRMATIONS

I have the expertise and creativity to overcome all problems.
I graciously receive help from others.

EVENING AFFIRMATIONS

I am a creative and artistic person.
I focus on what is best in every situation.

DAY 182

MORNING AFFIRMATIONS

It is easy for me to do all the difficult things.
I am always willing to go the extra mile.

EVENING AFFIRMATIONS

I have everything I need to live a great life.
I am willing to face and overcome all my fears.

DAY 183

MORNING AFFIRMATIONS

I keep getting better and better every single day.
I am grateful that today I am getting another chance to make a
difference in the world.

EVENING AFFIRMATIONS

Challenges always bring out my greatest strengths.
I enjoy changes and adapting to new situations.

DAY 184

MORNING AFFIRMATIONS

I am deeply content and happy with my life.
Every day in every way, my life keeps getting better.

EVENING AFFIRMATIONS

All my thoughts and actions are aligned with my life purpose.
I am concentrating all my thoughts on the results I want to manifest.

DAY 185

MORNING AFFIRMATIONS

Today, I am choosing to focus on the good in myself and in others.
My 'reality' is more beautiful than my dreams.

EVENING AFFIRMATIONS

I have faith that there is a solution for every problem.
I am prosperous and abundant in every way.

DAY 186

MORNING AFFIRMATIONS

I trust that everything is unfolding according to the plan the Universe
has for my life.
I am always surrounded by love and beauty.

EVENING AFFIRMATIONS

Creating my dream life is entirely in my own hands.
I am enough for myself.

DAY 187

MORNING AFFIRMATIONS

I am extremely gifted and talented.
I am always in a good mood.

EVENING AFFIRMATIONS

I take full responsibility for what I am thinking, feeling, and
experiencing in my life.
My goals and my desires are worth pursuing.

DAY 188

MORNING AFFIRMATIONS

Everyone loves me for who I truly am.
I always let my authentic self shine through.

EVENING AFFIRMATIONS

I have what it takes to be successful.
I am at peace being the person that I am.

DAY 189

MORNING AFFIRMATIONS

I am determined to turn all my dreams into reality.
I am completely in charge of my destiny.

EVENING AFFIRMATIONS

I am kind to myself.
I treat myself with thoughtfulness and consideration.

DAY 190

MORNING AFFIRMATIONS

I am ready to fully unleash my greatness.
I have been born to do incredible things.

EVENING AFFIRMATIONS

I am choosing to trust my intuition.
My intuition is always attuned with the truth.

DAY 191

MORNING AFFIRMATIONS

Being the best version of myself is my favorite project.
I am choosing to transform all my past hurts into pure love.

EVENING AFFIRMATIONS

I am a very important and valuable person.
I have the ability to learn and grow from all my mistakes.

DAY 192

MORNING AFFIRMATIONS

I choose to do my best in all situations.
I always aim high and get what I want.

EVENING AFFIRMATIONS

I always stay calm and collected.
I am a very practical and rational person.

DAY 193

MORNING AFFIRMATIONS

I am choosing to transform all my fears into faith.
Every day of my life is filled with miracles.

EVENING AFFIRMATIONS

I have the ability to bravely handle every life situation.
I am a person with integrity and values.

DAY 194

MORNING AFFIRMATIONS

I know that wonderful things are going to happen today.
I am ready to experience miracles today.

EVENING AFFIRMATIONS

My life is beautiful and rewarding.
I am always optimistic and hopeful for the future.

DAY 195

MORNING AFFIRMATIONS

Today, I am going to step out of my comfort zone to do something
different and new.
There are no limitations because all limitations are illusions.

EVENING AFFIRMATIONS

I am flexible and accommodating.
I keep an open mind to explore new opportunities.

DAY 196

MORNING AFFIRMATIONS

Problems are just opportunities in disguise.
Life is bringing me wonderful experiences that I thrive upon.

EVENING AFFIRMATIONS

Changes are wonderful and exciting.
I adjust and adapt to changing life situations with ease.

DAY 197

MORNING AFFIRMATIONS

Today I am going to live up to my full potential.
Today I'll give my best to every task I undertake.

EVENING AFFIRMATIONS

I am good at everything that truly matters to me.
I have unique gifts through which I make the world a better place.

DAY 198

MORNING AFFIRMATIONS

I am an infinite being having a temporary human experience in this
finite world.
My true self is limitless and boundless.

EVENING AFFIRMATIONS

I know that I am here on this planet for a reason.
I am worthy of love and respect exactly the way I am.

DAY 199

MORNING AFFIRMATIONS

It is easy for me to say no to everything that feels uncomfortable.
I set firm and strong boundaries for myself.

EVENING AFFIRMATIONS

Everyone treats me with respect and kindness.
I have the confidence and the courage to speak up for myself.

DAY 200

MORNING AFFIRMATIONS

I am a very hard working person.
I am an excellent learner.

EVENING AFFIRMATIONS

I have all the qualities of an outstanding leader.
I inspire others by my own example.

DAY 201

MORNING AFFIRMATIONS

I am making constant progress towards my goals.
I am ready to experience the fulfillment of all my dreams.

EVENING AFFIRMATIONS

Kindness comes naturally to me.
I am very comfortable in my skin.

DAY 202

MORNING AFFIRMATIONS

This world is truly a wonderful place.
I find innumerable well wishers wherever I go.

EVENING AFFIRMATIONS

I talk positively and kindly to myself.
My heart is always filled with gratitude.

DAY 203

MORNING AFFIRMATIONS

My capacity for greatness is infinite.
I am releasing all my worries and embracing positivity.

EVENING AFFIRMATIONS

I'm an honest and dependable person.
I have the courage to face all my fears and overcome them.

DAY 204

MORNING AFFIRMATIONS

It's always mind over matter for me.
My mind is stronger than my circumstances.

EVENING AFFIRMATIONS

I can handle everything that comes my way.
I have mastered the art of turning adversity into opportunity.

DAY 205

MORNING AFFIRMATIONS

Today is the first day of the rest of my life.
I can change my life in whatever way I want.

EVENING AFFIRMATIONS

Fortune always favors me.
Whenever I really want something, I get it.

DAY 206

MORNING AFFIRMATIONS

I'm ready to honor all my feelings and needs.
Today I am choosing to prioritize myself.

EVENING AFFIRMATIONS

I attract positive and happy people into my life.
I am exactly where I need to be at this moment in time.

DAY 207

MORNING AFFIRMATIONS

I am feeling calm and peaceful.
I am optimistic about the future.

EVENING AFFIRMATIONS

I am enjoying outstanding health and fitness.
It is fun being the best version of myself.

DAY 208

I'm extremely talented and creative.
I am really good at finding solutions for everything.

EVENING AFFIRMATIONS

I am the only one who can make me happy.
I always choose joy, happiness, and laughter.

DAY 209

MORNING AFFIRMATIONS

I believe I have been born for greatness.
I am choosing to think positive thoughts about myself.

EVENING AFFIRMATIONS

I am responsible for everything I am experiencing right now.
The power to change my life and my destiny is in my own hands.

DAY 210

MORNING AFFIRMATIONS

I respect and value my own opinions.
Other people respect and value my opinions.

EVENING AFFIRMATIONS

It is easy for me to be honest and authentic.
I am choosing to be serene and calm.

DAY 211

MORNING AFFIRMATIONS

I am feeling vivacious and vibrant today.
I have a radiant and glowing face.

EVENING AFFIRMATIONS

It is the journey that matters and not the destination so much.
I am enjoying the journey of life.

DAY 212

MORNING AFFIRMATIONS

I deserve beautiful relationships.
My loving presence is truly a gift to others.

EVENING AFFIRMATIONS

All my decisions are rooted in great self-respect.
I am good at setting loving and compassionate boundaries.

DAY 213

MORNING AFFIRMATIONS

I am doing my best, and that's what truly matters.
I am choosing to feel positive and confident.

EVENING AFFIRMATIONS

I feel safe within myself.
I am accepting and embracing all aspects of my personality.

DAY 214

MORNING AFFIRMATIONS

I know I am a very special person.
I love how unique and different I am.

EVENING AFFIRMATIONS

I am proud of the man/woman that I am.
My love for myself is boundless and limitless.

DAY 215

MORNING AFFIRMATIONS

My heart is always overflowing with love and gratitude.
I have limitless potential for experiencing growth and abundance.

EVENING AFFIRMATIONS

I have come into this world to succeed.
I'm always winning at the game of life.

DAY 216

MORNING AFFIRMATIONS

My strength increases with every step I take forward.
I know I am a strong and capable man/woman.

EVENING AFFIRMATIONS

There is beauty and blessing in every situation.
I am releasing all my inhibitions and hesitations.

DAY 217

MORNING AFFIRMATIONS

Today I am excited to live and express my true self.
I am going to live this day with boldness and kindness.

EVENING AFFIRMATIONS

Everything today has been just perfect.
It is easy for me to live in the present.

DAY 218

MORNING AFFIRMATIONS

Today I am choosing to rise above all my fears.
I am bold, outgoing, and confident.

EVENING AFFIRMATIONS

I dream about the future while keeping myself grounded in the present.
I approach all my goals with creativity and persistence.

DAY 219

MORNING AFFIRMATIONS

Confidence comes naturally to me.
I feel comfortable in all social and professional situations.

EVENING AFFIRMATIONS

I have a solutions mindset. I am a natural problem solver.
I am outstanding at finding the best solution for every problem.

DAY 220

MORNING AFFIRMATIONS

I like changes. I easily adjust and adapt myself to new situations.
I am always attracting favorable situations and amazing people into my
energy field.

EVENING AFFIRMATIONS

I have mastered the art of delayed gratification.
I am willing to forgo short-term pleasure for long-term success.

DAY 221

MORNING AFFIRMATIONS

I know I can master any skill.
I am outstandingly talented.

EVENING AFFIRMATIONS

I love being me.
I know there can never be another me.

DAY 222

MORNING AFFIRMATIONS

I have the intelligence and the skill to master anything.
There is no such thing as failure – Either I win or I receive an education.

EVENING AFFIRMATIONS

I gain something wonderful out of every situation.
My life is eternally blessed.

DAY 223

MORNING AFFIRMATIONS

The beauty of my soul shines brighter than the brightest diamond.
I enjoy keeping myself well-groomed and presentable at all times.

EVENING AFFIRMATIONS

I am willing and open to try new things.
My life is incredibly blissful and fulfilling.

DAY 224

MORNING AFFIRMATIONS

I deserve everything amazing.
I am my own greatest support system.

EVENING AFFIRMATIONS

I demand and accept nothing but the very best from myself and from life.
I am truly a legend.

DAY 225

MORNING AFFIRMATIONS

I am obsessed with personal growth and self-development.
I enjoy finding new and improved ways of doing things.

EVENING AFFIRMATIONS

I thrive on change and challenges.
I am constantly rebuilding a finer and more formidable version of myself.

DAY 226

MORNING AFFIRMATIONS

I rejoice in my freedom making my own unique choices and decisions.
My dreams are turning into reality very easily and effortlessly.

EVENING AFFIRMATIONS

I am one with the Universe and the flow of life.
I am giving up all resistance and struggle.

DAY 227

MORNING AFFIRMATIONS

I love how much people respect and adore me.
Everyone is always so happy to help me.

EVENING AFFIRMATIONS

I feel heard, acknowledged, and respected wherever I go.
I really like how attentively people listen to me every time I speak.

DAY 228

MORNING AFFIRMATIONS

I have a beautiful heart.
I am a truly beautiful person in every way.

EVENING AFFIRMATIONS

I am completely at peace with my life.
I trust that everything is going according to the divine plan for my soul.

DAY 229

MORNING AFFIRMATIONS

The Universe supports me every step of the way.
The Universe has got my back.

EVENING AFFIRMATIONS

I am fully accepting my inner and outer beauty.
I truly am divinely beautiful.

DAY 230

MORNING AFFIRMATIONS

I understand that growth is infinite.
I enjoy learning and growing.

EVENING AFFIRMATIONS

As long as I am making progress, I am doing well.
I feel I am a very successful person.

DAY 231

MORNING AFFIRMATIONS

I fully believe that success is a choice.
I keep working hard until I get what I want.

EVENING AFFIRMATIONS

The best things come to those who believe in their own greatness.
Greatness is in my genes. I have been born to be great.

DAY 232

MORNING AFFIRMATIONS

Every challenge I face brings out the best in me.
I believe I have the talent, intelligence, and power to succeed.

EVENING AFFIRMATIONS

I am a creative genius.
I am very good at finding the answer to every question that comes up in
my mind.

DAY 233

MORNING AFFIRMATIONS

I have the power to create and live my dream life.
My faith in myself and in my abilities keeps getting stronger every day.

EVENING AFFIRMATIONS

The Universe is infinitely abundant and plentiful.
There is ample in the world for everyone.

DAY 234

MORNING AFFIRMATIONS

I choose to focus on the beauty of life.
I choose to keep myself looking my best every day.

EVENING AFFIRMATIONS

I give my body, mind, and soul plenty of rest.
I like to take the time to relax and just 'be.'

DAY 235

MORNING AFFIRMATIONS

I dare to do the things that others shy away from.
My life is ruled by passion and love.

EVENING AFFIRMATIONS

I am ready to fully embrace the perfection of my soul.
I am perfect the way I am. Others are perfect the way they are.

DAY 236

MORNING AFFIRMATIONS

I am ambitious and hardworking.
Every morning, I wake up excited to live another amazing day of life.

EVENING AFFIRMATIONS

Today, I am choosing peace and contentment.
I feel happy and grateful to be me.

DAY 237

MORNING AFFIRMATIONS

I love every part of my body.
I love the reflection I see in the mirror.

EVENING AFFIRMATIONS

I like thinking and saying nice things about myself.
I enjoy making other people feel good about themselves.

DAY 238

MORNING AFFIRMATIONS

I have the mental toughness to get through anything in life.
I enjoy living a disciplined life.

EVENING AFFIRMATIONS

I believe in delayed gratification.
I am honoring my true self by fully accepting who I am at this moment.

DAY 239

MORNING AFFIRMATIONS

I am truly one of a kind.
I am a beautiful human being.

EVENING AFFIRMATIONS

I have a heart of gold.
I enjoy being kind and gracious.

DAY 240

MORNING AFFIRMATIONS

I enjoy nourishing my body with healthy food.
Exercising is a lot of fun.

EVENING AFFIRMATIONS

I am a fun person to be around.
I enjoy having a good time with my loved ones.

DAY 241

MORNING AFFIRMATIONS

My life is filled with divine grace.
The Universe supports all my dreams.

EVENING AFFIRMATIONS

I am always feeling enthusiastic, confident, and motivated.
I go to bed with the conviction that I already have everything I will ever
need or could possibly want.

DAY 242

MORNING AFFIRMATIONS

I enjoy wearing nice clothes that reflect my real personality.
Taking care of myself is fun and pleasurable to me.

EVENING AFFIRMATIONS

I always have energy to do the things that are important to me.
Even at the end of the day, I feel energetic and lively.

DAY 243

MORNING AFFIRMATIONS

I have very high energy levels.
My energy levels stay consistent throughout the day.

EVENING AFFIRMATIONS

I am attracting all the right people into my life who are aligned with my
life path and purpose.
I know and understand my life purpose perfectly well.

DAY 244

MORNING AFFIRMATIONS

I know I am worthy and deserving.
I believe I am a really nice person.

EVENING AFFIRMATIONS

I recognize my capabilities.
I am capable of doing things that no one else would dare to do.

DAY 245

MORNING AFFIRMATIONS

I follow my own lead.
I do what feels right to me.

EVENING AFFIRMATIONS

I have my own approval and that's what really matters.
I am grateful to be physically, mentally, and emotionally healthy.

DAY 246

MORNING AFFIRMATIONS

I am exceptionally fit and healthy.
I trust my heart and do whatever feels right to me.

EVENING AFFIRMATIONS

My body is amazing.
I feel beautiful/handsome inside and out.

DAY 247

MORNING AFFIRMATIONS

I thrive under all circumstances.
I know I am stronger than I think and smarter than I realize.

EVENING AFFIRMATIONS

My intuition always guides me in the right direction.
I always find the best solution for every challenge.

DAY 248

MORNING AFFIRMATIONS

I am determined to make today great.
I am extremely charismatic and irresistible.

EVENING AFFIRMATIONS

I like meeting new people and forming new friendships.
Everyone in my life enjoys my company.

DAY 249

MORNING AFFIRMATIONS

I strive for excellence in all areas of life.
I choose to hold myself up to a very high standard.

EVENING AFFIRMATIONS

It is easy for me to let go of anything that is not aligned with my soul's
purpose.
I joyfully accept that which I cannot change.

DAY 250

MORNING AFFIRMATIONS

I walk with confidence.
I always hold my head high.

EVENING AFFIRMATIONS

My self-respect is the most important thing for me.
It is easy for me to connect with others.

DAY 251

MORNING AFFIRMATIONS

I treat myself like royalty.
I am a queen/king.

EVENING AFFIRMATIONS

I feel good being totally myself.
I have the courage to express my authentic self under all circumstances.

DAY 252

MORNING AFFIRMATIONS

I am feeling and expressing boundless joy.
My faith in my greatness is growing with every passing day.

EVENING AFFIRMATIONS

I treat my body as my best friend.
How I am living each day is entirely in my own hands.

DAY 253

MORNING AFFIRMATIONS

I feel youthful, energetic, and vibrant.
It is easy for me to get whatever I desire.

EVENING AFFIRMATIONS

The kindness of my soul reflects in my countenance.
Everyone knows that I am a genuinely wonderful person.

DAY 254

MORNING AFFIRMATIONS

I am always willing to start over from scratch.
No matter how many times I have to do it, I know I can always build
back better.

EVENING AFFIRMATIONS

I work hard to make every day my best.
I am choosing to be one with the flow of life.

DAY 255

MORNING AFFIRMATIONS

My happiness is in my own hands.
It is easy for me to think good thoughts about myself and about others.

EVENING AFFIRMATIONS

I live my life like royalty.
I always conduct myself with grace, poise, and elegance.

DAY 256

MORNING AFFIRMATIONS

I smile easily and effortlessly.
Everyone loves my smile.

EVENING AFFIRMATIONS

My life is a success story.
People feel inspired by me.

DAY 257

MORNING AFFIRMATIONS

I am a wonderful person with good intentions.
People see me as noble, kind, and gracious.

EVENING AFFIRMATIONS

I have a magnanimous heart.
I enjoy blessing others in whatever way I can.

DAY 258

MORNING AFFIRMATIONS

Today I am accepting only good thoughts and good wishes in my energy
field.
I trust I have the power and the ability to realize all my goals.

EVENING AFFIRMATIONS

I am grateful for all the good that surrounds me at this very moment.
Serenity is my natural state of being.

DAY 259

MORNING AFFIRMATIONS

I take long and relaxed deep breaths.
I am always at ease no matter where I am.

EVENING AFFIRMATIONS

I am reclaiming my power as a powerful divine being.
I can shape my destiny however I desire.

DAY 260

MORNING AFFIRMATIONS

I have the skills and the knowledge to handle any situation effectively.
I want only the best out of life and out of myself.

EVENING AFFIRMATIONS

I pay the price for what I want through hard work and persistence.
I know how perfect every day of my life really is.

DAY 261

MORNING AFFIRMATIONS

I enjoy giving love and hugs.
I love myself from the core of my heart.

EVENING AFFIRMATIONS

My heart is warm and beautiful.
I treat others with respect, kindness, and consideration.

DAY 262

MORNING AFFIRMATIONS

I am in touch with my intuition.
I am choosing to hear the whispers of my intuition that echo in the
recesses of my heart.

EVENING AFFIRMATIONS

The beauty of life amazes me every single day.
I am grateful to be alive in this day and age within this time and space.

DAY 263

MORNING AFFIRMATIONS

I am here to touch lives and to make the world a better place in my
own way.
I am choosing to acknowledge and honor the calling of my soul.

EVENING AFFIRMATIONS

I enjoy keeping my space organized and beautiful.
I always think calm, peaceful, and positive thoughts.

DAY 264

MORNING AFFIRMATIONS

Being calm and peaceful is my superpower.
I know I can find the solution to everything when I am calm and
peaceful.

EVENING AFFIRMATIONS

My life is unfolding in perfect harmony with the Universe's plan.
I am a powerful human being.

DAY 265

MORNING AFFIRMATIONS

Every single day, I strive to live my life as fully as possible.
I make my own rules.

EVENING AFFIRMATIONS

I have full autonomy over my body, mind, and spirit.
I am answerable only to myself and the divine within me.

DAY 266

MORNING AFFIRMATIONS

I live life with a sense of humor.
There is joy to be found even in the unlikeliest of circumstances.

EVENING AFFIRMATIONS

I am here on this planet to fully realize my destiny as an incredible
human being.
My presence brings light and hope to this world.

DAY 267

MORNING AFFIRMATIONS

Today I am choosing to focus on what is pleasant and beautiful.
My heart is always overflowing with joy.

EVENING AFFIRMATIONS

I am relaxed and at ease with life.
I trust that everything is unfolding exactly as it should.

DAY 268

MORNING AFFIRMATIONS

I have kind and compassionate eyes that see the good in others.
I use my lips to smile and speak soothing words.

EVENING AFFIRMATIONS

Inside my heart, I already have all the love that I can ever need.
I am fully in touch with my heart's true desires.

DAY 269

MORNING AFFIRMATIONS

I accept change.
To keep growing, I keep changing and evolving for the better.

EVENING AFFIRMATIONS

I take all my responsibilities very seriously.
I am fully committed to fulfilling my responsibilities.

DAY 270

MORNING AFFIRMATIONS

I am a man/woman of my word.
When I say I will do something, I just do it.

EVENING AFFIRMATIONS

It is easy for me to keep myself motivated at all times.
I have excellent daily habits that influence my behavior positively.

DAY 271

MORNING AFFIRMATIONS

I carry myself with excellent posture throughout the day.
My self-confidence is reflected in my excellent posture.

EVENING AFFIRMATIONS

I have the power and conviction to stand up for what matters to me.
I am an exceptionally talented and capable person.

DAY 272

MORNING AFFIRMATIONS

I show others how to treat me by always conducting myself with self-respect.
I am someone who is respected and revered by others.

EVENING AFFIRMATIONS

It doesn't matter how many times I fall down, I always get up.
I always come back stronger and more powerful than ever before!

DAY 273

MORNING AFFIRMATIONS

My heart is always singing with joy.
I find happiness in all situations and under all circumstances.

EVENING AFFIRMATIONS

I always take the time to properly chew and fully enjoy the food I am eating.
I savor and relish every moment of life.

DAY 274

MORNING AFFIRMATIONS

I choose to always hold on to hope.
I am always hoping for the best in every situation.

EVENING AFFIRMATIONS

Good things happen to good people, and I am a really good person.
I am always looking and feeling amazing.

DAY 275

MORNING AFFIRMATIONS

I am ready to get the best out of life today.
I am feeling light, relaxed, and completely at ease.

EVENING AFFIRMATIONS

My heart is fully healed of all past traumas.
Today I am forgiving everyone who I believe has wronged me.

DAY 276

MORNING AFFIRMATIONS

I know I have everything I need to make today a success.
The best things in life come to me easily and effortlessly.

EVENING AFFIRMATIONS

I trust that everything is completely under control.
I can conquer any and every life situation.

DAY 277

MORNING AFFIRMATIONS

I have infinite reserves of strength.
I am gliding through life with deep inner peace in my heart.

EVENING AFFIRMATIONS

I know how to be gracious while also setting strong boundaries.
I feel safe and secure with where I am in life.

DAY 278

MORNING AFFIRMATIONS

I have the courage to be open and vulnerable with my loved ones.
My relationships with others are beautiful and satisfying.

EVENING AFFIRMATIONS

I always find something to be grateful for.
My blessings keep growing every day by leaps and bounds.

DAY 279

MORNING AFFIRMATIONS

I am very good at making the time to do the things that really matter
to me.
I eat all my meals with a peaceful mind and a calm heart.

EVENING AFFIRMATIONS

I am completely supported by the Universe in every way possible.
I am a calm and peaceful person.

DAY 280

MORNING AFFIRMATIONS

I have a sharp mind and a loving heart.
I enjoy smiling and laughing.

EVENING AFFIRMATIONS

I trust that every event and situation in my life is taking me closer to my
dreams.
I always choose faith over fear.

DAY 281

MORNING AFFIRMATIONS

My competition is only with who I was yesterday.
I feel happy for and cheer on others who are doing well.

EVENING AFFIRMATIONS

I like sharing other people's happiness.
I am always seeking to learn from those who have what I want for
myself.

DAY 282

MORNING AFFIRMATIONS

I am the only person who has power over me.
I can always choose to respond positively to any situation.

EVENING AFFIRMATIONS

I like taking the time to nurture my body, mind, and soul.
I enjoy following a healthy daily regime.

DAY 283

MORNING AFFIRMATIONS

I have the power and autonomy of choice in every situation.
I am really good at making pragmatic choices.

EVENING AFFIRMATIONS

I am accepting myself fully and completely exactly the way I am.
It is easy for me to see the best in myself.

DAY 284

MORNING AFFIRMATIONS

All the forces of the Universe are working in my favor.
My awesomeness keeps growing every day.

EVENING AFFIRMATIONS

I enjoy living life at the highest potential of my soul.
Greatness is my birthright. I am claiming it right now!

DAY 285

MORNING AFFIRMATIONS

I am an extremely productive and results-oriented person.
I am a top performer.

EVENING AFFIRMATIONS

I keep growing in wisdom every single day.
I use my time and energy wisely.

DAY 286

MORNING AFFIRMATIONS

Every moment of life is bringing out the best in me.
I am a happy, secure, and trusting person.

EVENING AFFIRMATIONS

I can see through people very easily.
I am allowing in my energy field only those who have my best interest at
heart.

DAY 287

MORNING AFFIRMATIONS

My presence alone can illuminate any room.
People feel uplifted in my presence.

EVENING AFFIRMATIONS

I deserve beautiful and fulfilling relationships.
Everyone in my life recognizes the fact that I am a wonderful person.

DAY 288

MORNING AFFIRMATIONS

I light up the room with my smile.
I have a bewitching and mesmerizing smile.

EVENING AFFIRMATIONS

I know how to have a good time and help others have a good time.
I am the type of person everyone loves being around.

DAY 289

MORNING AFFIRMATIONS

I am the only person who gets to decide my self-worth.
I am a rare and incredible person.

EVENING AFFIRMATIONS

I am constantly upgrading myself and my skills.
My life can only get better and more beautiful.

DAY 290

MORNING AFFIRMATIONS

It is my duty and obligation to be a massively successful person.
In my eyes, I am an incredibly successful person.

EVENING AFFIRMATIONS

I receive blessings wherever I go.
People always give me the very best of who they are and what they have.

DAY 291

MORNING AFFIRMATIONS

I am always investing in myself and expanding my skill set.
The only person I compete with is the person I see in the mirror every
morning.

EVENING AFFIRMATIONS

I am happily embracing and accepting my flaws.
I strive to be better while fully accepting and loving who I already am.

DAY 292

MORNING AFFIRMATIONS

I pay close attention to the needs of my body.
I give ample rest to my body, mind, and soul.

EVENING AFFIRMATIONS

I can always begin again and build back better.
I am proud of everything I have accomplished.

DAY 293

MORNING AFFIRMATIONS

I am grateful for every person I have met and every circumstance I have
been through.
I won't be who I am today if my life hadn't panned out exactly the way
it has.

EVENING AFFIRMATIONS

Every day, I take the time to slow down and simply be.
I have truly mastered the art of living beautifully.

DAY 294

MORNING AFFIRMATIONS

I am grateful for my true friends and well-wishers who want only the
best for me.
I am exceptional at everything I do.

EVENING AFFIRMATIONS

Things always pan out better than I can imagine.
My life is full of pleasant and beautiful surprises.

DAY 295

MORNING AFFIRMATIONS

I am an incredibly blessed person.
My dreams are materializing faster than I realize.

EVENING AFFIRMATIONS

In my world, everyone is wonderful, beautiful, and kind.
I know how to make other people feel appreciated and loved.

DAY 296

MORNING AFFIRMATIONS

I am always at home in every environment.
I am an easy-going and fun-loving person.

EVENING AFFIRMATIONS

I always have time to eat all my meals in peace.
With every passing minute, I am feeling calmer and more peaceful.

DAY 297

MORNING AFFIRMATIONS

I am smart with how I use my resources.
My time is my most valuable resource. I spend it carefully and wisely.

EVENING AFFIRMATIONS

I am strong and independent.
I enjoy being truly self-reliant and self-sufficient.

DAY 298

MORNING AFFIRMATIONS

I have the power and the ability to fulfil all my needs.
I take pleasure and pride in looking after myself.

EVENING AFFIRMATIONS

If something doesn't work out, it is because there is something much
better waiting for me.
I have a strong support system around me in the people who truly care
for me.

DAY 299

MORNING AFFIRMATIONS

I always attract good people into my energy field.
I perform each task with hundred percent focus and dedication.

EVENING AFFIRMATIONS

I persist and persevere no matter what.
People see me as a legend – a truly exceptional person.

DAY 300

MORNING AFFIRMATIONS

I deserve wonderful experiences.
There is magic in every moment of life.

EVENING AFFIRMATIONS

My life has meaning and purpose.
I go to bed feeling content and at peace with myself.

DAY 301

MORNING AFFIRMATIONS

I receive admiration and adoration wherever I go.
I can easily handle any situation.

EVENING AFFIRMATIONS

How blessed am I!
I have a bewitching and captivating smile.

DAY 302

MORNING AFFIRMATIONS

I am choosing to focus on only the beautiful memories from the past.
What's not a beautiful memory is simply an important learning
experience.

EVENING AFFIRMATIONS

I am an avid learner.
I have an intense hunger for knowledge and wisdom.

DAY 303

MORNING AFFIRMATIONS

I have mastered the art of being firm while also being gentle.
I am a very graceful and poised person.

EVENING AFFIRMATIONS

I smile brightly and whole-heartedly.
I have lived a truly perfect day today.

DAY 304

MORNING AFFIRMATIONS

I am a first class version of my highest self.
I seek to be extraordinary and exceptional in every way.

EVENING AFFIRMATIONS

I dare to live every day of life on my own terms.
I am bold enough to let my true self shine in all circumstances and
places.

DAY 305

MORNING AFFIRMATIONS

Good people are naturally and powerfully drawn to me wherever I go.
It is easy for me to exercise emotional control at all times.

EVENING AFFIRMATIONS

I am a passionate person.
I am a benevolent, kind, and compassionate person.

DAY 306

MORNING AFFIRMATIONS

I am strongly motivated, passionate, and determined.
My presence is a gift to the world.

EVENING AFFIRMATIONS

I am grateful to my life's journey and everything it has taught me.
I shine each day – thanks to my internal motivation.

DAY 307

MORNING AFFIRMATIONS

I am always high on life.
I know how to get the nectar of wisdom and growth out of any
situation.

EVENING AFFIRMATIONS

I am very good at recognizing and capitalizing on opportunities.
It is easy for me to love others because I truly love myself.

DAY 308

MORNING AFFIRMATIONS

I am worthy of having everything I want.
The entire Universe is conspiring in my favor.

EVENING AFFIRMATIONS

I ask for help whenever I really need it.
People truly enjoy helping me.

DAY 309

MORNING AFFIRMATIONS

My life is overflowing with miracles and blessings.
My daily habits are in perfect harmony with my ultimate life purpose.

EVENING AFFIRMATIONS

I show up and give my best every day of life.
Positive people and positive circumstances find me wherever I go.

DAY 310

MORNING AFFIRMATIONS

I know how to recognize and maximize opportunities.
I have full control over my thoughts and my feelings.

EVENING AFFIRMATIONS

I am perfectly at ease with the flow of life
I am embracing all my life lessons with gratitude.

DAY 311

MORNING AFFIRMATIONS

I am feeling inspired, motivated, and happy.
Everything is possible in my world.

EVENING AFFIRMATIONS

I always come up with the most brilliant ideas.
Everything I can ever want is already within my reach.

DAY 312

MORNING AFFIRMATIONS

I have an abundance mindset.
I believe we can all be successful, wonderful, and happy at the same time.

EVENING AFFIRMATIONS

I enjoy giving genuine compliments to others.
I graciously receive compliments from others.

DAY 313

MORNING AFFIRMATIONS

With every challenge I overcome, I am becoming better and wiser.
I am fully responsible for all my life experiences.

EVENING AFFIRMATIONS

Anything I can ever want is already mine.
I know how to turn my dreams into reality.

DAY 314

MORNING AFFIRMATIONS

I am constantly exploring my own infinite reserves of strength.
I am a brave and intrepid person.

EVENING AFFIRMATIONS

I enjoy adventurous new experiences.
I am very comfortable with stepping out of my comfort zone.

DAY 315

MORNING AFFIRMATIONS

I have mastered the art of letting go and moving on from the past.
I hear the voice of my heart loud and clear.

EVENING AFFIRMATIONS

I believe in the essential goodness of all human beings.
I truly believe that everyone is good at the core of their being.

DAY 316

MORNING AFFIRMATIONS

Every hurdle I face increases my ability to jump higher.
I can only get stronger and smarter.

EVENING AFFIRMATIONS

I can always find the truth inside my own heart.
I am comfortable in my own company.

DAY 317

MORNING AFFIRMATIONS

I am surrounded by miracles and magic at this very moment.
My life is unfolding beautifully and perfectly.

EVENING AFFIRMATIONS

I am very good at nurturing all my important relationships.
I know how to make people feel special, admired, and loved.

DAY 318

MORNING AFFIRMATIONS

I am embracing the mystery and beauty of life.
Today is going to be the best and most perfect day of my life.

EVENING AFFIRMATIONS

I find the seed of joy and gratitude in every situation.
The fact that I am alive at this time on this planet is itself a great miracle.

DAY 319

MORNING AFFIRMATIONS

I am very good at turning theoretical knowledge into practical application.
Today, I am choosing to be my best self – strong and confident.

EVENING AFFIRMATIONS

I am a true gentleman/gentlewoman.
I influence others with my kindness and love.

DAY 320

MORNING AFFIRMATIONS

I am a deeply spiritual person.
I am obsessed with being the best version of myself.

EVENING AFFIRMATIONS

I have mastered the fine art of positive and uplifting conversations.
I have the ability to say the right things at the right time to the right people.

DAY 321

MORNING AFFIRMATIONS

I am super excited for this new day and all the wonderful opportunities that are coming my way.
I trust that all my dreams are materializing in perfect divine timing.

EVENING AFFIRMATIONS

I am choosing to fully relax and let the Universe do its work.
I know exactly what I want with complete clarity.

DAY 322

MORNING AFFIRMATIONS

I cherish and value all my loved ones.
It is easy for me to give and receive love.

EVENING AFFIRMATIONS

I am worthy of all the compliments and appreciation I receive.
I am a highly respected person in all spheres of life.

DAY 323

MORNING AFFIRMATIONS

I find beauty and joy in the simple things of daily life.
I have a keen eye for aesthetics and beauty.

EVENING AFFIRMATIONS

I am confident and proud of my beautiful body.
I have the strength to say no when something doesn't serve my highest
good.

DAY 324

MORNING AFFIRMATIONS

I perform all my tasks with commitment and joy.
My performance in every area of life is top notch.

EVENING AFFIRMATIONS

It is easy for me to achieve success.
I persist and persevere until I succeed.

DAY 325

MORNING AFFIRMATIONS

I am radiant, effervescent, and confident.
People are magnetically drawn to my exuberance and zest for life.

EVENING AFFIRMATIONS

I see opportunities where others see problems.
I have the unconditional love and acceptance of the people who matter
most to me.

DAY 326

MORNING AFFIRMATIONS

I am always cheerful and jovial.
I greet everyone with a sincere smile on my face.

EVENING AFFIRMATIONS

I have the right to live life on my own terms.
I always play by my own rules.

DAY 327

MORNING AFFIRMATIONS

I like serving others in my own way.
The more I focus on giving, the more abundant and wealthier I become.

EVENING AFFIRMATIONS

I keep breaking my own records.
I know I can do even the most impossible things.

DAY 328

MORNING AFFIRMATIONS

I trust my ability to overcome all adversities.
There is a smooth and infinite flow of abundance in my life.

EVENING AFFIRMATIONS

I pat myself on the back every time I do something well.
I constantly keep learning new things.

DAY 329

MORNING AFFIRMATIONS

I am going to do everything that it takes to make this day my best.
My inner power keeps growing every day.

EVENING AFFIRMATIONS

I speak with sincerity and honesty.
My words soothe and heal the hearts of people.

DAY 330

MORNING AFFIRMATIONS

I am a spiritual being enjoying a temporary stint of human life.
No matter what happens in this life, my soul is immortal, infinite, and
eternal.

EVENING AFFIRMATIONS

My spiritual beauty shines through my physical body.
I inspire others to be their best self.

DAY 331

MORNING AFFIRMATIONS

I wake up with excitement and enthusiasm every day.
I am very good at being productive and getting things done.

EVENING AFFIRMATIONS

I have the potential for extraordinary success.
I am enjoying living life at the peak of success.

DAY 332

MORNING AFFIRMATIONS

I am a very understanding and empathetic person.
I always strive to understand others without judgment.

EVENING AFFIRMATIONS

Acting with integrity is a high priority for me.
I am choosing to be serene and peaceful.

DAY 333

MORNING AFFIRMATIONS

I choose my words with care.
I believe in benevolent honesty.

EVENING AFFIRMATIONS

I respect the feelings and sentiments of others.
By being kind, I keep enhancing the beauty of my soul.

DAY 334

MORNING AFFIRMATIONS

The only person I compare myself with is who I was yesterday.
I know how to be a giving person while also honoring my own needs.

EVENING AFFIRMATIONS

I am a success because I am better than who I was yesterday.
Every day brings with it a chance to start afresh.

DAY 335

MORNING AFFIRMATIONS

I am free from all regrets of the past and fears of the future.
I have mastered the art of living in the moment.

EVENING AFFIRMATIONS

I constantly keep pushing myself out of my comfort zone.
To be truly alive, I must keep constantly growing.

DAY 336

MORNING AFFIRMATIONS

I am living a life of deep fulfillment and great rewards.
I spend my days doing the things I absolutely love doing.

EVENING AFFIRMATIONS

I strive to always stay true to my soul and my life purpose.
I have depth, intensity, and intelligence.

DAY 337

MORNING AFFIRMATIONS

Integrity is my hallmark.
I put my heart and soul into everything I do.

EVENING AFFIRMATIONS

I know how to be loving and kind to myself.
My standards for myself are extremely high.

DAY 338

MORNING AFFIRMATIONS

I know how to be fully present in each moment.
I do everything with mindfulness – being fully present in body, mind, and spirit.

EVENING AFFIRMATIONS

My life becomes better and more beautiful when I help others improve their lives.
I generously share my knowledge and wisdom with others.

DAY 339

MORNING AFFIRMATIONS

I always know what the right thing to do is in any situation.
I have the courage and conviction to do the right thing in every situation.

EVENING AFFIRMATIONS

My heart is blooming with gratitude for the innumerable blessings in my life.
I am in love with my life.

DAY 340

MORNING AFFIRMATIONS

I always like to give myself the VIP treatment.
I am the most important person in my life.

EVENING AFFIRMATIONS

I know how amazing I am!
I say only the best things about myself and about others.

DAY 341

MORNING AFFIRMATIONS

I always put my own oxygen mask first before helping others.
Catering to my own needs is always a top priority for me.

EVENING AFFIRMATIONS

I am excellent at time management.
I know how to make the best and most efficient use of the 24 hours I
have in a day.

DAY 342

MORNING AFFIRMATIONS

I always act with discernment and good judgment.
I am taking full responsibility for all my actions.

EVENING AFFIRMATIONS

I write down all my goals and create clear action plans for achieving
them.
Faith combined with hard work is my mantra for living a good life.

DAY 343

MORNING AFFIRMATIONS

My dream life is already mine.
All my goals are fully aligned with my core values and personal beliefs.

EVENING AFFIRMATIONS

Daily self-care is an absolute necessity for me.
I keep myself well hydrated and well fed at all times.

DAY 344

MORNING AFFIRMATIONS

I have healthy skin and hair.
I enjoy taking good care of my skin and hair.

EVENING AFFIRMATIONS

I practice daily self-reflection and constant self-analysis.
I am always looking for ways to become better.

DAY 345

MORNING AFFIRMATIONS

I am open to new and innovative ways of thinking.
I am always willing to explore and try new more efficient ways of doing
things.

EVENING AFFIRMATIONS

I witness all my thoughts without judgment and attachment.
I understand that I am not my thoughts – I am only a witness to their
ebb and flow within my mind.

DAY 346

MORNING AFFIRMATIONS

I am in touch with my true needs, wants, and desires.
I know how to ask for what I want from others in a kind and gracious
manner.

EVENING AFFIRMATIONS

I am making a positive impact in the world.
I always treat others with kindness and consideration.

DAY 347

MORNING AFFIRMATIONS

I have the ability to take constructive criticism.
I ignore all negative criticism.

EVENING AFFIRMATIONS

I firmly believe in the greatness of my own soul.
I choose to be truly myself in all situations.

DAY 348

MORNING AFFIRMATIONS

I am boldly embracing the beauty of life.
Today is a perfect day to live and thrive.

EVENING AFFIRMATIONS

I have access to infinite abundance.
My strength and power keeps growing every day.

DAY 349

MORNING AFFIRMATIONS

I always act with courage and kindness.
I confidently and courageously stand up for myself.

EVENING AFFIRMATIONS

I am a gifted person.
I become more abundant by sharing my blessings with others.

DAY 350

MORNING AFFIRMATIONS

I wake up every morning energized and refreshed.
I have unique and extremely valuable gifts to share with the world.

EVENING AFFIRMATIONS

I have a powerful sense of self.
I believe in myself irrespective of anyone else's opinion of me.

DAY 351

MORNING AFFIRMATIONS

I attract in my energy field only those people who truly respect me and
appreciate who I am.
My well-wishers are always showering me with genuine praise and
appreciation.

EVENING AFFIRMATIONS

I am a champion!
I like doing the difficult things that make my life easier in the long-run.

DAY 352

MORNING AFFIRMATIONS

Self-discipline comes naturally and effortlessly to me.
I have the mindset and self-discipline of a champion.

EVENING AFFIRMATIONS

I am confidently charging ahead in the direction of my dreams.
I have full faith in my skills, abilities, and intelligence.

DAY 353

MORNING AFFIRMATIONS

I trust that I can handle anything.
I know how to turn my weaknesses into strengths.

EVENING AFFIRMATIONS

I believe in a bright and beautiful future.
I am very humble and extremely confident at the same time.

DAY 354

MORNING AFFIRMATIONS

I like being good to people.
Other people are always kind and generous towards me.

EVENING AFFIRMATIONS

Every experience of life is helping me grow and evolve.
I am thriving in all aspects of my personal life.

DAY 355

MORNING AFFIRMATIONS

I am always relaxed and calm in all situations.
I have a soothing and powerful voice.

EVENING AFFIRMATIONS

I like socializing with others.
I can talk to anyone with confidence.

DAY 356

MORNING AFFIRMATIONS

I feel really good about myself and my life.
Every day is a fresh start.

EVENING AFFIRMATIONS

I am grateful for how successful today has been.
I am falling asleep with a content heart.

DAY 357

MORNING AFFIRMATIONS

I take care of my body by eating healthy and exercising regularly.
I have power and autonomy over my future.

EVENING AFFIRMATIONS

I am truly fortunate, lucky, and blessed.
My life is exactly the way it should be.

DAY 358

MORNING AFFIRMATIONS

I know how to treat others with compassion and understanding.
My kindness is always well received and well reciprocated.

EVENING AFFIRMATIONS

My daily regime is fully aligned with my larger purpose.
I have a crystal clear vision for what my future looks like.

DAY 359

MORNING AFFIRMATIONS

I live every day of my life with discipline and quiet confidence.
I feel confident because I believe in myself.

EVENING AFFIRMATIONS

I am filling my mind with positive thoughts and wonderful ideas.
I believe only good things can happen to me.

DAY 360

MORNING AFFIRMATIONS

I believe I am exceptional in every way.
I do everything with great love and passion.

EVENING AFFIRMATIONS

I rely on the wisdom of my own heart for guiding my life decisions.
I am determined to make the best use of my time and energy.

DAY 361

MORNING AFFIRMATIONS

I have the most wonderful family and friends.
I receive unconditional love and support from my loved ones every step
of the way.

EVENING AFFIRMATIONS

I am fully present in this moment.
I am exceptionally strong, brave, and resilient.

DAY 362

MORNING AFFIRMATIONS

I can achieve anything that I truly want.
By focusing on keeping myself happy, I am able to make others happier.

EVENING AFFIRMATIONS

I am in love with the person that I am and the person that I am
becoming.
I am choosing to surround myself with kind and supportive people.

DAY 363

MORNING AFFIRMATIONS

My desires and goals are worthy of being pursued.
My comparison and competition is only with myself.

EVENING AFFIRMATIONS

I am loving and kind to the person I meet in the mirror every day.
When I do something for others, it is always from my heart.

DAY 364

MORNING AFFIRMATIONS

I receive positive vibes wherever I go.
I stay in high spirits all day.

EVENING AFFIRMATIONS

I'm always striving to be the finest version of myself.
I always do the best that I am capable of.

DAY 365

MORNING AFFIRMATIONS

I am a very responsible person.
I take full responsibility for my life.

EVENING AFFIRMATIONS

I am a brave and daring soul.
I am comfortable taking risks.

BONUS AFFIRMATIONS

Now that you have come to the end of the year-long journey, here are some bonus affirmations to help you continue the practice for another 10 days. Just remember – the more frequently you practice affirmations, the greater your mastery over them will be.

MORNING AFFIRMATIONS

I find pleasure and joy even in the simplest everyday things.
I aspire for greatness in all life situations.

EVENING AFFIRMATIONS

The Universe is always bringing me pleasant surprises.
I am always willing to put in the time and effort to get what I want.

2

MORNING AFFIRMATIONS

My health and wellbeing is always my topmost priority.
Right now, I am choosing inner peace.

EVENING AFFIRMATIONS

I trust that the final outcome is always going to be in my favour.
I am experiencing one favorable circumstance after another.

MORNING AFFIRMATIONS

I am grateful to all the people who have contributed towards my success.
I can get anything if I truly want it.

EVENING AFFIRMATIONS

There is great joy in the simple things of everyday life.
I am choosing to feel calm, content, and peaceful.

#4

MORNING AFFIRMATIONS

My heart is overloaded with joy.
I am freeing myself from all doubts and fear.

EVENING AFFIRMATIONS

I am convinced that I am here in this world to do something great.
I stay calm no matter what is happening in the world around me.

MORNING AFFIRMATIONS

I use my best things every day because I truly deserve it.
I like to dress my best every day because then I also feel my best.

EVENING AFFIRMATIONS

My heart is an infinite reservoir of unconditional love.
I like showering my loved ones with affection.

#6

MORNING AFFIRMATIONS

As a champion, I am always hungry for more.
Today I am living my perfect day.

EVENING AFFIRMATIONS

I take the time to understand and appreciate other people's perspectives.
It is easy for me to earn other people's respect.

MORNING AFFIRMATIONS

I am comfortable with being deeply loved and admired.
I am holding on to my vision of a better, more beautiful future.

EVENING AFFIRMATIONS

My calmness and serenity keeps me anchored in the present moment.
Thanks to my faith in myself, I just keep moving forward.

8

MORNING AFFIRMATIONS

I am my own savior.
The only person who can give me what I desire is me.

EVENING AFFIRMATIONS

I peacefully fall asleep every night.
My heart is illuminated with unconditional love.

9

MORNING AFFIRMATIONS

I take care of myself very well.
I know how to cater to the needs of my loved ones while also
prioritizing my own needs.

EVENING AFFIRMATIONS

Things just keep getting better every day.
I think and feel positively about myself.

MORNING AFFIRMATIONS

I take consistent action to turn my goals into reality.
I constantly keep improving my talents and skills.

EVENING AFFIRMATIONS

I am devoted to progress and personal development.
As long as I am growing and becoming better, I am successful.

A SHORT MESSAGE FROM THE AUTHOR

Hey, are you enjoying the book? I'd love to hear your thoughts!

Many readers do not know how hard reviews are to come by, and how much they help an author.

I would be incredibly grateful if you could take just 60 seconds to write a brief review on Amazon, even if it's just a few sentences!

Thank you for taking the time to share your thoughts!

Your review will genuinely make a difference for me and help gain exposure for my work.

S. S. Leigh

CONCLUSION

Thank you for taking this journey with me into the wonderful world of affirmations. I really hope that this has been a life-changing experience for you. Practicing affirmations is such a powerful tool for bringing about long-lasting inner transformation as it is our thoughts that create and dictate our reality.

To change your circumstances and create the reality you desire, you have to master your thoughts. When you are intentionally focusing on those thoughts that are aligned with the reality you want to create and experience, then it is inevitable that the Universe will eventually bring you what you desire.

As is the case with any skill, consistency is the key here. You must stay consistent with your practice of affirmations. Practicing them every morning and evening is crucial but you also must incorporate them throughout the day. Instead of seeing them as something you have to do twice a day, you must internalize affirmations to the point that they become an essential component of your everyday life.

Whenever a negative thought arises, counteract it immediately with a positive affirmation. If you can nip destructive negative thoughts in the bud, then they will never get a chance to materialize in your reality. Never forget that this world is only a shadow of your imagination. What you imagine in your mind is always what you get to experience in your reality. Again, I am not talking about what you think you desire and what you would like to believe you always imagine but those images and emotions that spring forth from the deepest recesses of your subconscious mind.

Affirmation is a tool that can scrape off and clear the debris of unwanted thoughts and beliefs from your subconscious mind. The catch is you have to practice affirmations with consistency, dedication, and commitment to the point that they become one with your identity.

Wishing you a beautiful journey ahead into the 'reality' of your fulfilled desires!

Sincerely,

S. S. Leigh

Made in the USA
Middletown, DE
07 May 2023

30161665R00086